Jacky Newcomb is the UK's leading expert on the after-life, having dedicated her life to the subject. She is a *Sunday Times* bestselling author with numerous awards to her name, a regular columnist for *Take a Break*'s *Fate & Fortune* magazine, and is a regular on ITV's *This Morning*, Lorraine Kelly's show and C5's *Live with Gabby*.

Also by Jacky Newcomb:

A Gift from Heaven

A Gift from Heaven

True-life stories of contact from the other side

Jacky Newcomb

Harper
True *Fate*

A few details have been changed to protect the privacy
of the individuals concerned.

HarperTrueFate
An imprint of HarperCollins*Publishers*
77–85 Fulham Palace Road,
Hammersmith, London W6 8JB

www.harpertrue.com
www.harpercollins.co.uk

First published by HarperTrueFate 2014

1 3 5 7 9 10 8 6 4 2

Jacky Newcomb asserts the moral right to
be identified as the author of this work

A catalogue record of this book is
available from the British Library

ISBN: 978-0-00-810508-2

Printed and bound in Great Britain by
RR Donnelley at Glasgow, UK

Chapter 1

Gone but Still Here

One of the most exciting things this book will reveal to you is that even though a person has passed away, they are still alive. If you haven't read any of my books before, this may be the point at which you say, 'OK, this woman is crazy,' but I promise I am not. Let me explain: many millions of people have experienced contact from their loved ones ... *after* the physical body has passed away. And I'm not just talking about people who visit psychics or, to be honest, people with any real belief in an afterlife at all. The deceased are simply popping back from heaven to say hello and let us know they have survived death in some way.

It's true that the physical body ceases to exist, but somehow the spirit or the soul of that person, complete with their earthly personality, continues to survive. Over the years, I've loved sharing these true-life stories in my books and articles. Some would say that my life mission is to continue to do so – and I'm inclined to agree with them.

Many of the experiences in this book are one-offs; in other words, the person receiving the contact hasn't experienced anything like it before and may never experience such contact again. Others, like me, have been lucky enough to have contact from loved ones on the heaven side of life over and over again. Let me give you some examples.

Terry got in touch with me from Australia to tell me about his encounter with the other side. He was just eighteen when his experience happened. One day, after his dad had passed away, he was sitting up in bed, wide awake, when his father walked into the bedroom. He just appeared through the doorway and sat on the bed. Terry said the whole experience was bizarre but he felt no fear, just amazement. His dad was surrounded by light, which Terry found fascinating, and the pair of them just chatted together for a long time. He'd visited, he said, because he wanted to reassure his son.

Terry's late father communicated a message to him, saying, 'Don't be afraid to die, Terry. It's so easy. Look, I will show you what happens.' The spirit then split in two in front of his son and both of the separate parts said, 'Now you do it!' Terry feels that at this point his father must have helped him somehow to do the same, as his own spirit body separated from his physical body, but he didn't feel afraid as this happened. As Terry looked at his dad he noticed that his father's eyes shone with bliss and love. Then the two halves of his dad's body merged back together again and simply walked back out the way he had come! Terry knew that he hadn't dreamt this because he told me he was very aware of being awake; this makes the experience all the more remarkable.

But, of course, Terry is not the only one to have an unusual encounter with the afterlife. Jayne is from England. She told me that her nan passed away about nineteen years ago; a couple of weeks before she died, Jayne gave birth to her youngest son, Jack. Jayne recalls that her nan was well enough to see the baby and hold him, even though it was only once, before she passed away.

Jayne was so upset at the loss of her nan, and she was having a bad time in other areas of her life, too, because she was also dealing with a violent partner. One night she went to bed but woke again in the early hours of the morning; something felt different in the room, she recalls. She normally had her bedroom door closed, but when she looked towards the door it appeared to be wide open. It was very bright – much brighter than a normal light. Then Jayne noticed a figure appearing. She also said she didn't feel afraid at all for some reason. She just kept watching, but at the same time felt calm. Jayne soon realised it was her nan in the doorway, and her nan was looking at her. Suddenly she was really close, right up by the bed, and looking down on her, smiling. Jayne says at that moment she knew that things would work out OK, and she drifted off to sleep again.

Then one night, about a month after seeing her nan, Jayne had a strange 'dream'. She found herself in a park, sitting on a bench, and her nan was with her again. Jayne said, 'I can't remember the whole conversation, but I can remember she said, "I can't stay long; I will have to go soon. You will be OK. Things will get better."' Jayne's nan then said good-bye and drifted away.

Her nan appeared several more times after that but only when Jayne was feeling low. Then, a few months later, she finally found the courage to split up with her partner and things did get better. Jayne feels that her nan made her realise that it was the right thing to do, and although she doesn't see her as much now, she still feels that if she really needed her nan, she wouldn't be very far away.

There is something special about knowing that our loved ones are still around for us when we need them. It's comforting to know that they are aware of the struggles and worries we are going through, even though they are not physically in our lives. They have the ability to check in from time to time to soothe and reassure us. Has a deceased loved one visited you in this way?

There have been numerous studies on afterlife phenomena over the years. One was conducted by a

British doctor, W. D. Rees, who contacted a sample group of widows in Wales. Of these, 47 per cent believed they'd had afterlife contact (sometimes over and over again, continuing for a number of years) from their deceased husbands. That's quite a high figure, isn't it? I think it shows this phenomenon is perhaps more normal than paranormal.

Many visitations occur in an unexpected form, such as this next one, which happened to Nicky. She explained that her partner passed last year, and he sent birds to her when she wasn't paying attention to him – meaning that she felt he'd been trying to reach out to her and she hadn't noticed. Nicky was in shock the first week after her partner died because his death was so sudden and unexpected. She says the birds literally came right up to her and looked like they were trying to speak – they kept opening their beaks with no sound coming out!

When the initial shock wore off, Nicky could hear her partner saying things like, 'You need to eat something,' or, 'Go inside, it's cold now.' As time went on she could hear messages more clearly, and on a couple of occasions she felt the physical touch of him as he took hold of her hand. Nicky's children have also felt his presence and heard him speak to them. They've also had dream visitations from him, so here is one man who was determined to let his family know he had survived physical death in some way. This is not as uncommon as you would think. After my own dad passed on, his children and great-grandchildren all had visitation experiences; he was a regular 'dream visitor'.

Birds have played a part in numerous afterlife contact stories that I've read over the years. Wild birds seem especially friendly, tapping on the window to get your attention, hanging around for days on end or even sitting on people's hands! Maybe you've experienced contact in this way, too? I've been going through a challenging time in my own life recently, and last week a little bird twice came and knocked on the window. I was shocked the first time and he flew away fairly quickly, but the second time I was ready. I sat open-mouthed as he tapped away for several seconds. I wanted to call out for my husband to witness what I was seeing but didn't want to frighten the bird away. The bird stuck around long enough for me to have taken a photograph of him on my phone, but for some reason I had left my phone downstairs when it's normally next to me on my desk. Perhaps the action would have spoiled the magic somehow. Maybe I was meant to experience the moment, rather than waste time taking a photograph (a life lesson, I'm sure).

Lynn's experience was much more direct. She was lucky enough to have a very real chat with a loved one from the other side. She told me her grand-mother passed away in 2012. A few weeks after she passed, Lynn was walking up the stairs when she saw her grandmother at the top. As if that wasn't strange enough, that night Lynn had a dream: her grandmother was in her bedroom. Lynn spotted her so went in to join her and sat down on the bed. Lynn was confused and questioned how her grandmother was able to be back with her even though she had just passed over. The woman replied that she was not staying long but that she'd just popped back to give her granddaughter a hug. The pair hugged for a few moments, and Lynn says she sobbed with grief as she explained to her grandmother how much she missed her. The woman was aware of this and was sympathetic but explained that she wasn't going far and would always be around for the family.

This encounter follows the classic 'visitation format', where the experience is so real and we are so lucid that we are confused as to why they (the spirits of the deceased) can visit us when they are 'dead'. The spirit looks and feels like a normal, living human being during the course of the visitation. Although it's rare to be able to touch the deceased, it does happen, and it's happened to me numerous times: a loving hand in your hand, a touch on the shoulder or a full-on hug. They are very precious gifts from heaven. Lynn's visit was a short one, as they normally are. It seems it's difficult for the spirit to 'hold' this shape and stick around in this mutual location for long periods of time.

Lynn continued with her story and said her gran then had to leave, even though she didn't want her to. She begged the woman to stay, but she became very stern. She got up, walked her to the door and said strongly, 'YOU ARE NOT COMING WITH ME! You have work to do.' With one last hug, her gran parted with the words, 'I love you, chicken.' Then she shut the door firmly.

Lynn cried for her grandmother to let her in but there was no reply, and when she tried the door it wouldn't open. Lynn woke up with tears rolling down her cheeks and knew the experience was real; it left her with a warm feeling. Her gran has been back a few times since and Lynn loves it when it happens. She often appears during normal dreams and the pair always share a hug.

It might seem as if Lynn's grandmother was pretty strict in this experience but this, too, is a classic part of the encounter. To 'stay' for any length of time would mean that Lynn would have to pass over too, and of course that is not allowed! The deceased always tell us it's not 'our time' and that we have many more things to do on earth (lessons to learn, help to give others and so on). Our lives – and the plan for our future life – impact upon many others along the way. A smile we give to a stranger might one day save someone's life, or being in a particular place means we introduce a friend to their future partner, and so on. If we leave too soon it interferes with many more lives than our own. Our loved ones want us to visit with them, not cross over to heaven with them!

My own father visits me in dream-visitation experiences occasionally. I love it when Dad holds my hand because it feels real in the way it did when he was in his physical body. I often cry, too. I miss Dad and want to stay with him, but of course I want him back on this side of life rather than having to go to his side – not yet, anyway! It's strange to wake up and know those tears are real and feel them running down your face.

I've also had visitation hugs. They feel completely normal, in the same way they did when he was on earth. In a recent visitation experience I had my hands on a door and recall the sensation of the handle most clearly. Even during the dream experience I remember thinking, 'Wow, that feels completely real!' It's the lucidity of the encounter that makes you realise this is no ordinary dream. We interact with the people who visit, whereas in a normal dream the action is often muddled and disconnected.

Occasionally people drop into deep meditative states or dream-sleeps, where they visit these afterlife realms. I know there are websites where folk can learn to have these experiences on purpose so that they can see more of the other side. It's not easy! I've tried, with limited success. If you want to have a go at this, search using the phrase 'out-of-body experience' or 'OOB/OOBE'. I reached the stage where I could lift my spirit body out of my physical body and float around the house. Occasionally I'd travel further and have bigger experiences almost by accident. You can read more about my out-of-body adventures in my book *An Angel Saved My Life*. This is certainly an interesting technique to learn if you are bedridden or bound to a wheelchair. The freedom you feel during the out-of-body experience is amazing and certainly worth investigating!

Donna visited the other realms by accident, too. She told me that when she was around ten, she recalls falling asleep one night and all of a sudden she found herself walking along a golden path. There were millions of flowers on either side. She was on a mission, following the path somewhere, and all around the light seemed golden. She could see other people too, but they looked like shadows on the path.

Then she turned and looked up and was aware of her spiritual self looking down at the person on the path below. Suddenly she was pulled up by 'Big Nana' (her great-nana, who passed over some while before). The woman was lifting her out of bed really fast and really high. Then the next thing she recalls was being back in her bed and Big Nana was sitting beside her. 'She died when I was very young,' Donna told me, 'but I still knew it was her.' The experience remains just as clear to her today as it did back then, and she still recalls all the details and emotions that she felt at the time.

I love to read about the 'geography' of heaven, and I once wrote a book full of descriptions of the other side. When you see how many people independently visit the afterlife and then come back and share the same visions, it makes you realise that these experiences have to be real. Heaven is a wonderful world full of light and amazing colour. Anyone who sees these magical realms comes back with the feeling of wonderful, unconditional love.

Other encounters with the afterlife take place very much in our world. Carole's experience involved a physical interaction that makes it extra special. She explained how she had lost her lovely dad fifteen weeks before writing to me; they'd made a pact twenty-five years earlier that whoever went first would bring contact from the other side. Since her dad had passed on, Carole had been very down and ill. She went to a spiritual church a few times, and although her friend had messages from her own mum who'd passed, there was nothing there for Carole, and she naturally felt disappointed.

Then recently she was feeling depressed and ill once again and lay down on the settee, thinking a little snooze would be helpful. About an hour later she woke up absolutely freezing. The rain was lashing against the windows but she didn't have time to move her body because all of a sudden her dad was by her side. He looked just as he had a few years before, when he was still alive, Carole recalled. He reached across and pulled a blanket over his daughter and even tapped her shoulder comfortingly, as if to say, I'm here still, and then he went. Since that afternoon she's become more aware of him and it's really helped her adjust to the situation. Carole is so pleased her dad kept his word to appear to her after he passed away.

Carole then contacted me again a few months later with some more sad news. In January, when the weather was at its worst, her ten-month-old kitten went out and never came back again. Naturally she was devastated. But then she woke up to see a faded outline of her dad holding the kitten and she felt relieved. Dad had also brought the dog (that she'd lost the year before to old age) with him. Carol feels she had the proof she was looking for. Not only was she comforted to know that her loved ones had continued to live, but they were also together.

What a sad story! But it's nice to know that the kitten and the dog are safely with Carole's dad. After my dad passed, he visited me and my sisters in dream visitations with different pets on different occasions! He still sometimes has a dog with him when he visits. So many people want to know that their pets, which are so important to us in life, are also safe after death. It's essential for us to know that they, too, made it safely to the afterlife. After many, many years of writing these books and sharing true-life stories, I know it's real. Yes, pets go to heaven too! Do you have pets on the other side? I know you'll feel as reassured by this phenomenon as I do.

I personally love it when psychic phenomena happen too – do you know what I mean? My dad and uncle were big doorbell ringers after they passed on; it was one of their many ways of letting us know they were around. I find all that exciting, but I'll admit that most people are frightened by physical activity. However, it's less scary when you are on the verge of sleep, either just before waking or just before falling asleep. Janie had this happen to her recently. She explained that she'd just come back from her best friend's funeral. Janie called her friend her angel because she was so caring to her and others. One night she went to bed crying, and when she finally got to sleep a light woke her up again. She heard a whisper in her ear saying, 'You know you used to call me your angel? Well, I am!' Janie heard a chuckle and the light went again. What a lovely experience.

With afterlife experiences like this we have to remember that the love we shared on the earth side of life doesn't suddenly disappear after our loved ones pass on. When they come back to visit from the other side they bring that same love with them and their personalities are much the same. If Uncle Bob didn't frighten you when he was alive, he certainly isn't going to scare you now he is dead (at least, he doesn't mean to!).

Actually, this is a good place to say that if someone did hurt you in life and they do try to come back to see you, it's because they have a wider perspective and understanding of what they did wrong now that they are a spirit. They would only be coming back to say sorry (and yes, this does happen from time to time). Of course, the same rules apply in heaven as they do on earth. Just because someone comes knocking at the door, it doesn't mean you have to let them in! If you are worried that someone you disliked (or were frightened of) might come back from the other side, let me reassure you that they may not do so without your permission. You can ask your own guardian angel to bar the way, or imagine the great Archangel Michael (the one you see in churches) standing guard with his great sword. Say no and they have to go away. This is a great way of empowering yourself and getting back your strength against someone who hurt you in life. You're in charge now.

If you're new to this phenomenon and it all sounds a little crazy, let me reassure you once more. This isn't some made-up New Age mumbo jumbo – this information comes from real-life experiences that my readers have shared with me. Lots of people (especially children) experience Archangel Michael in dream visitations! (For some children, they actually see Michael – or Mike – when they are awake.) You are perfectly safe. Over the years, lots of people have written about spirits who came back to apologise to them. You can ask the angels to hold that person at arm's length if you feel the need. However, you might find a little peace if the spirit does come back to apologise in a way they were unable to do in life. Give it some thought. Your forgiveness might help you both to move on.

Chapter 2

The Dream Visitation

When I first began writing my true-life-story books about angels, people from all over the world began sending me their own experiences. It didn't take long before I realised that their experiences began to fall into two distinct categories. Category one was the classic angel experience. The angel appeared as a being of light, a creation of God, a protector and guardian of humankind, during times of trouble or when people were grieving, sick or perhaps involved in a serious accident. Sometimes people saw a full-blown angel figure manifest in front of them; other times a mysterious stranger held their hand and comforted them until help could arrive. In almost every situation, the 'angel' would disappear mysteriously. These angels usually left the person with a deep sense of peace and comfort. They were unlike anything people had experienced before – or were they?

Then there was a whole other set of experiences. These involved visits from the deceased: our loved ones appearing to us in times of trouble, when we are sick, to comfort us ... well, you get the idea. Our loved ones were acting *as if* they were angels too, and were reaching out from the other side of life in a similar way. They appeared as themselves but usually at their best: shining, full of vitality and healthy, and sometimes looking like angels (I think the shining light is the key here!).

Over time, these types of experiences became more and more prevalent, yet very little was written about the phenomenon. Some spirits brought signs that they were around (see my book *Messages from Angels*), but others came to visit directly, often in a very real visitation experience, either when the person was asleep or, occasionally, wide awake.

Although we call them dream visitations, they are not dreams. They seem to happen during the dream cycle of sleep; in fact, often the receiver is actually dreaming at the time and then the dream scene slides away and the visitation begins. The visitation can be very brief or last a little longer. The short visitation experience may involve just a face appearing through a cloud or white light, and then fading away. This vision has so much meaning, even though it worries people. 'What did they want?' everyone asks me. 'What were they trying to say?'

Every visit means I love you, I am here for you, I am still with you ... I survived physical death! A visit from the other side is the most precious gift you can ever receive. It says, life continues after the physical body passes away. When you receive a visit from the other side, it's an experience that lasts your whole life long. You'll never forget that someone you loved was able to interact with you long after their physical body passed away. It takes time and effort for your loved one to visit in this way (we know how hard it is for us to reach out to them!). So a visitation encounter of this type is very precious indeed.

It doesn't matter that your body is asleep when the experience happens. During the encounter you'll be aware that your body is sleeping. You'll also be completely lucid while it happens; *you* are not asleep, even though your body is. On occasion I've even heard myself snore – how funny is that? During the whole visitation I've known that my body was asleep but that I, Jacky (the spirit of me), was completely aware and 'awake'. Unlike a dream, you'll be able to think as if you were awake. You'll talk to your visitor, usually expressing surprise that they are 'alive' and able to interact.

You'll ask questions. Sometimes people will ask the spirit, 'You realise you're dead, don't you?' And normally they do. Other times you'll ask questions about your family, and if the spirit can answer you it will. I've had occasions where I've been given the answer to important life questions and been reassured that everything will be OK. Sometimes the information is actually suppressed afterwards. It's like they want to tell us what happens next but, like in an exciting novel, they don't want to spoil the ending, or aren't allowed to – maybe because we need to work it out for ourselves, a life lesson to be learned.

The 'ending' of each chapter of our lives can vary depending on our actions. There are general trends set in life, but at any time we can live better lives if we choose. We have control over so many things: we decide on how well we treat our bodies (what we eat and how we exercise); we choose what sort of work we do, where we live, who our partners are and how positive (or not) we are about our lives. Has anyone ever told you that before? It was a strong lesson I received from the other side. So they may reassure us but leave the actual living of the event down to us. Always remember that you are the author of your own play – you write the lines you're going to live. So make sure it's a good one!

Spirits can help us but, in the end, we choose. Does that scare you or empower you? No psychic in the world can make you do anything at all. No spirit is in charge of you. Their messages come with love. They want the best for us, they want us to make good choices, but ultimately those choices and the lessons that go with them are ours to make. What things would you change about your future life knowing that you, and only you, are in charge?

You might be interested to know that as I typed that, a beautiful soft-grey pigeon (a messenger bird) flew right up to my window! It must be another one of those 'coincidences' we've been talking about! The word 'angel' means … messenger!

Afterlife communication: it's a real interaction with a real (spirit) being. After such contact you'll probably be changed for ever. Knowing that life continues after death affects how you live today. And that is the point. These messages reassure us that even though others have passed away, we should continue to live our lives to the fullest.

Chapter 3

Everything Is OK

Sometimes the primary reason for a visitation is simply to reassure the living that everything is going to be OK in the future. We as human beings spend so much time worrying about what might be, rather than living in the moment. To be fair, the loss of a loved one is different. It can be overwhelming. The thought of going on alone or without the helpful and loving influence of the recently departed is just more than people can cope with. The deceased sometimes visit just to let the living know that although they'll still feel the challenge, everything will work out OK in the end. Or, as the saying goes, if it's not OK yet then it's not the end!

After my dad passed away, my mum worried about money, and one night she stayed awake, crying. Dad appeared to me in a visitation dream to show me his old brown wallet, which was bulging with cash. He held it out to me as a sort of sign that there was 'enough'. He was right. After checking her finances, Mum had enough money to move into her new apartment, but while we, the family, were working out the figures for her, she was reassured knowing that Dad felt everything would be OK. It was, of course.

Here is a similar story from Sarah. She told me her granddad passed away in July 2009 and that same year she tragically miscarried a longed-for baby. Sarah felt like her heart had been ripped out. It was not her year. Don't you find it's harder to cope when more than one loss occurs in a short time? I know I do. I'm sure her granddad had this in mind when he found a way to reassure her.

In February 2010, she found out she was pregnant again. It was very exciting news, but of course she was concerned that something might happen to the baby again. Then, one night, about halfway through her term, her granddad came to visit while she was asleep. 'The dream was so real that I felt like I was awake when it happened,' says Sarah. Her granddad appeared in a familiar way and looked just how he'd appeared when he was alive and well. He was sitting in a brown high-backed old-style chair. He was smiling and holding a baby girl. He just kept smiling and looking at the baby. Then Sarah woke up and no one was there. Yet the change had been made and she was completely reassured.

Sarah says she knew it was her granddad telling her that everything was going to be OK, and from the dream she understood that the baby was to be a girl. Granddad was right! Several months later, Sarah gave birth to a beautiful healthy little girl, but when she told her family about the experience, they didn't really believe her and explained the incident away, saying that it was because she used to think about Granddad a lot. Sarah didn't mind; she knew it was real, and she told me she remembers it just as clearly today as when it happened. It doesn't matter that people don't believe, because she knows Granddad is looking after her!

If you've been lucky enough to have a visitation experience of this type, don't worry if people don't believe you or tell you that you are hallucinating or something similar. I've written piles of books full of stories like these – you know you're not alone. Be assured. The phenomenon is very real indeed.

Sometimes the visit is simply a reassurance that another relative who has passed on is OK too. Tracey explained that she was at the lowest she had ever been when she first contacted me after her mother died, but was grateful that I emailed right back with positive thoughts. Apparently, shortly after my email she started to notice that someone was with her. She said she could not see the person, but one night a light started to appear under the door. Tracey felt 'different' somehow while this was happening and bravely went to the door, but found the light almost too bright. Right away she said she knew her mother was standing behind her. Tracey couldn't stop crying and in her head she heard a voice tell her it was her 'Mam'. Tracey's mother explained that it was time for Tracey to let her move on. She reassured her that she would always be with her and that she was just a thought away.

Tracey's mother continually reassured her that she was loved and that heaven was a wonderful place to be. Then the light faded. Tracey says it was strange but it never occurred to her to turn round that whole time, and that it was almost as if time stood still during the experience.

It's great when our loved ones can just let us know they are still around. This next story includes a pet visit, too. Joy explained that her husband, Roger, passed over last June and has appeared to her three times since. One night she awoke to find him kneeling down so his face was level with hers, which was on the pillow. He looked so excited and vibrant, and she could feel his energy. The last time, she awoke, or seemed to wake, to see him standing at the bottom of the bed, and she said, 'I love you.' He reminded her of the first LP, by Nat King Cole, that he had bought Joy when she was seventeen.

Joy went out to the local pub with her children to discuss her first day at a new job, and when they mentioned Daddy, the light above them in the little booth flashed. They laughed and said he must be listening in to their conversation. I remember my own sister talking to some friends about afterlife contact and they, too, were sitting in a booth at a pub. The disbelieving friends were unconvinced, but then a lampshade above the table suddenly fell to the table between them. I think the friends were convinced!

Joy's experience continued with a dream. She was on a beach by the sea, with all the family. When the sun started to set, the colours engulfed the whole scene in a rainbow-type kaleidoscope, which was really beautiful to behold. These extra rainbow colours, or 'very vivid' colours, come up again and again in afterlife visits. You'll notice, too, how bright lights are a common theme.

Joy went on to tell me what happened when she was nursing Roger at home. 'During the last few days he said he could feel Max (our yellow Labrador) brushing past his leg,' she said. Max had passed over fifteen or so years earlier, and she knew the old dog would be excited to see Roger once more.

She also remembered six or seven years earlier, getting up in the night to use the bathroom and suddenly finding Max in there with her. She bent down to embrace him, saying, 'Max, it really is you, isn't it?' when he disappeared. This was shortly before she had to have a pacemaker fitted as an emergency procedure. Maybe the dog appeared to reassure her.

There are several interesting points to note about these experiences. I love that Roger brought his wife the memory of special music they'd enjoyed. I laughed when I read about the lights flashing. That happens a lot at my mum's house when we talk about my late father or her partner who passed over recently. We also say, 'Oh, "so-and-so" must be listening to our conversation!' I imagine them sitting in the empty armchair and it's almost as if they are joining in. The lights flash not only when we mention their names, but also when we discuss something they most certainly would have agreed with. It's like they're saying, 'Here, here!'

The rainbow experience has come up a lot in previous stories of the afterlife. During near-death experiences people say that at the point where their spirit body reaches heaven (or close to it), they see colours that they have never seen on earth. Heavenly colours are always described as vibrant and rainbow-like; sometimes people tell me that the colours themselves have a sort of living energy to them.

Here is another example of a spirit communicating with a loved one to let them know they are OK. Barbara had a terrible shock, but it included a reassuring message. She explained that in December 1979 her sister Sallie died; she was only twenty-two. Her passing stunned the whole family, and is something her parents never seemed to recover from.

On the fateful day something very strange happened. Barbara was rushing back to work at lunchtime and was running a bit late. Just for a moment, she stopped to check the time and rear-range her shopping bags, and suddenly she was surrounded by a foggy haze. The noise from the traffic diminished to almost nothing, and a little bird was jumping and singing very close to her. The bird seemed to have no fear at all. It was all very unusual. Barbara happened to glance at her watch and noted that it was 1:20 p.m. Then the noise from the traffic came back, like someone turning the volume up on a TV; the haze and the bird disappeared, and she rushed back to the office.

Barbara recalls that it had been a very worrying few days because her sister Sallie had been taken ill and nobody seemed to know what was wrong. She was on life support in a London hospital. She arrived back home in the evening to the awful news: Sallie had died at 1:20 p.m. that afternoon – the exact time Barbara had her unusual experience.

That isn't the end of the story, though. Several days later Barbara woke early in the morning to see her sister Sallie standing by her bedside; she looked beautiful and so full of love and happiness. Barbara described to me a white light that somehow came from within her. Sallie held her sister's hand and told her why she had to die, as well as lots of other things that Barbara found wonderful at the time, even though afterwards she couldn't remember all the details (that can sometimes happen). Tears were running down her face. Her mind was trying to understand what was going on, and suddenly she became very scared. Sallie understood how Barbara felt and said, 'Don't worry, Babs, I'm all right.' And just as quickly, she was gone again. Like others before her, Barbara has never forgotten her experiences and knows it was not a dream.

When it comes to all of the details, sometimes they can get temporarily forgotten. Most of the dream visit remains clear and vivid for years to come, but when spiritual insights are shared it's like we are not meant to carry the details into our conscious memory. The information is either too overwhelming for our human brains or too pertinent to our own future life. The spirit of our loved one is able to help us, but there is a fine line between helping and interfering!

This may not make much sense, but let me try to explain. Imagine the spirit of a late relative says to you, 'Don't worry, it will all work out with you and Duggie.' Yet for you to fully learn your life lesson you need to split up with Duggie and go out with Jed for six months. Jed may not be your soulmate, but your interaction with him brings useful learning, which you need for your future life with Duggie. However, if the spirit tells you that it will work out with Duggie, you may then decide to persevere with your relationship as it stands, and those important insights never happen. So sometimes it's better to live your life without knowing too much!

During my own dad's visits in dreams, he sometimes 'gives me a clue' when I feel he wants to share something he isn't meant to. Good old Dad! I've been doing this for so long I can't imagine anything he had to tell me would make the situation worse! Naturally, as humans we don't want or need to know everything that is coming up. The loss of a loved one would be even harder if the death was to be sudden and unexpected (unexpected to us but not to the soul). I imagine if we knew six months in advance that someone was going to transition we'd just start mourning their loss for the whole six months beforehand! Spirit contact can be tricky.

One of the more challenging times after losing a loved one is when special occasions come around, like birthdays or anniversaries. The first one after a passing is particularly hard. To see the empty chair at the table, to know that the person will no longer be a part of those rituals they performed or participated in, is painful.

Janet contacted me after reading a previous book of mine. She was kind enough to let me know how much she enjoyed my work, and explained how she felt connected to the part where I'd explained that some souls need to rest or be healed after their passing. Janet felt that this phenomenon happened with her mother.

Janet's mum passed in September 2011, aged eighty-eight; it followed several years of poor health. They were very close and Janet still feels horribly lost without her. That Christmas she kept praying and saying that all she wanted was one last chance to hug her mum. Christmas Eve she dreamt of her. She was in a white room. A nurse was standing in front of the door and her mum was arguing with her. She kept saying that she had to leave because it was Christmas and she had to be with her children. In the dream, Janet rushed forward and wrapped her arms around her mother, and all the while she kept chanting over and over to her mother, 'I love you, I love you, I love you.' Her mum never acknowledged her presence and slowly faded away, but the whole time she continued saying that she had to leave. Janet was greatly comforted by her dream visitation, and even though her mother seemed unable to interact with her directly, she felt she'd been given her 'one last hug' as she'd requested.

Have you ever had an experience like this one? I think Janet might be right and that her mother was unable to interact with her directly because her own soul was healing, which made it impossible. I love that she did everything possible to still let herself be seen in this clever way. I often hear about spirits which, after passing, finding themselves in a hospital-type setting. I'm not sure the soul goes to a heavenly hospital, but rather a healing space. The hospital is familiar because it's something we know from our earthly lives. Seeing a nurse would be comforting, as we would know it meant we were being taken care of. What do you think?

Chapter 4

A Gift from Heaven

Every so often people receive a gift from the other side. I believe spirits are limited in what they can do to help us – they can't tell us what to do or solve problems that we must work out for ourselves – but if they can get involved then they will. I like to ask my angels for a few treats, especially when money is short. One day my husband and I were pretty broke and decided to take a trip to the local shopping centre. We enjoyed looking at all the pretty things, even if we couldn't actually afford to buy them. Then we walked into a new clothes shop and were handed a glass of buck's fizz each; it was an opening 'welcome-to-the-store' treat. It was just a small glass – a cocktail of fresh orange juice and sparkling wine – but it was very welcome, and free. Then we walked round the corner and someone was handing out free samples of fresh mixed juice (thank you very much!).

Later, we walked past a gorgeous patisserie. The window was full of wonderful cakes and pastries. We couldn't afford one of them but I had enough change to buy a couple of gorgeous truffles – one each. I complimented the manager on his wonderful window display and, as he was placing the chocolates into the bag, he said, 'Oh, I think I will give you two each rather than one,' but, of course, he still only charged us for one! There seemed no obvious reason why he should do this. Perhaps he was encouraged to do so by the angels.

Who knows whether that was angels or loved ones on the other side, but it was a great coincidence if it wasn't, right? Melanie wrote to tell me of a similar experience she had after a special dream. Her aunt gave her some gold in the dream and said the word 'birthday'. Melanie didn't know what she meant by it, but was delighted when she won £450 on her mother-in-law's birthday three days later! I wonder if Melanie bought something gold with her gift …

All visitation experiences are gifts in a way, but this one of Melanie's was extra special. It makes me wonder if spirits can manipulate the situation for us, or if they are limited to just sharing good news. Over the years people have told me how they had a dream of money coming to them, and then it did. Maybe that person needed the relief of knowing the money was on its way as much as they needed the actual cash. Being tight for cash can be stressful. Although we are spiritual beings we do have to live in the real world, and money, sadly, is how it all works.

Of course, money doesn't bring happiness, but it certainly has the power to make things a little easier. Tiny angelic treats, like my two extra chocolates, really make my day. They make me feel like everything is OK with the world. It seems daft, really. Why should something so simple make such a big difference? But it does! I always feel this way about feathers as gifts from angels. I've written about the white feather being a gift from an angel in several of my books. Indeed, the humble white feather might be the angels' biggest gift of all.

I was sitting watching the TV yesterday following a diagnosis at the doctor's (don't worry, medication will sort me out). Even though I know I'll be OK, I was still feeling a little sorry for myself. The cat (Tigger, my ginger tom) came and jumped up on my lap for a fuss. Why is it that pets always know when we need comfort? We snuggled up for a few minutes and then he jumped down again. I already felt better but then I noticed something sticking out of my trousers – yes, it was a white feather! Maybe the cat had it stuck in his own fur and transferred it to me when he sat on my lap. Who knows? But the timing, as always with angel feathers, was perfect.

Have you ever asked for a gift from heaven? Asking is certainly one of the keys to receiving. There is an unwritten rule that our angels (as well as our deceased loved ones) are not to interfere with our lives and choices on this side of life, but usually this isn't something we want them to do anyway. When times are difficult for us, when we are facing overwhelming challenges, what we want to know is that we are not alone. The traditional saying is that a trouble shared is a trouble halved, and what this basically means is that if you have someone you can talk to about your issues, you already feel better.

You don't need to worry about receiving a reply from heaven when you speak. Simply connect with your angel (or know deep inside that you have), or connect to the soul of a lost loved one. Imagine them clearly in your mind or, if you find that hard, look at a photograph as you do this. Ask that they walk beside you as you go through this difficult life lesson, whatever it might be. You may see your guardian in a dream or during meditation, or you might notice twinkling lights or unusual mists, as some people in this book have. Others just feel a change in the air around them. Time may appear to slow down momentarily, or you just get a strong feeling that someone is with you. Occasionally people receive a tangible sensation. For example, you might feel as if someone is literally touching your hand or placing a reassuring hand upon your shoulder. Be open to whatever comes and know that their intent is never to frighten you. These comforting signs always arrive with love. The point is to bring you joy or love, knowing that you are supported at all times by your angels on the other side of life.

In some of my other books I've talked about the gifts being physical – something you can literally touch or hold. One woman had a long-lost (very precious) necklace drop out of the air after she asked that it be returned. I had a missing earring, which mysteriously reappeared again overnight.

Spirits might move objects around to let you know they are with you during difficult times, or sometimes appear just before (sometimes moments before) bad news is announced. Other times their visits are more random (maybe they have recently learnt the phenomenon of visiting earth in their spirit body!)

They can't always bring back missing objects, but they might show you where the object is. I lost a gold wedding ring once (it belonged to a late aunt) and I was repeatedly told it was in a wooden box. The only wooden box I could think of was an old jewellery box my husband had by his bed – he kept his watches in it. There was a gold ring in the box but my husband insisted it had belonged to his late father. After getting frustrated I tried on the ring and it fitted me perfectly. We realised right away that it was way too small for a man's hand; the ring had ended up in the box by mistake, and the spirits had been correct all along.

People have asked for money to buy objects they needed, and although the money might not have appeared, the object might well have done. Years ago, when I had a young family and money was tight, I asked my angels to bring me money for food. While that didn't happen, people regularly invited us over for dinner or gave us tins and packets of food they didn't like or want. These gifts from heaven appeared in ways that were not expected, and that is another of the tricks from the other side. Our angels seem more likely to bring us what we need than what we ask for. If you look back at your own life, you may recognise many similar experiences.

When I was too poor to buy a coat, an elderly friend passed away and her daughter asked me if I knew anyone who might like three beautiful wool coats. The lady had exquisite taste and at least one of the coats looked like it had never been worn. Not one coat, but three, all different colours and lengths. It was like Christmas Day!

I hadn't used any special rituals to summon up these items, but I'd quietly requested them in my mind. By feeling confident that the items you need will arrive – maybe by saying something like, 'Thank you for solving my transport problem, angels' – you'll be surprised at how they can help you. In your mind you might be hoping for a brand-new sports car, but perhaps the angels know someone who is driving your way each day and would be grateful for someone to split the costs of the fuel with.

This technique seems to work just as well if you say it out loud. You can discuss it with a friend (the angels will hear you just the same). Tell them that you have a problem (and explain what it is), and that you are confident the angels will help you solve it. Why this can work so well is that your earthly friend may well have a solution for you. People love to solve other people's problems, and it's even easier to help someone who is positive and upbeat about a situation. Your friend might find him or herself 'spontaneously' asking around for you, perhaps speaking to their own friends and acquaintances to see if others might assist (not in the least influenced by the angels!). You might need a single bed for your spare room, and your friend works with someone who desperately needs to get rid of their 'little-used' guest bed because they are moving to a smaller house. You'd be doing them a favour and they'd be helping you out. I think angels must do a lot of matchmaking in this way, connecting people to solve problems.

How would you like angels to gift you at this moment in time? What challenges are you finding difficult to overcome on your own? At all times we want and need to solve our problems to learn our earthly lessons (we need to work it out for ourselves), but there is no rule that says a friend can't help another friend in need, is there? What is getting you down right now? Speak to your own angel right this very moment in your mind. Thank them for helping you solve your problem and then be ready for the answer to come to you in an unexpected way.

Sometimes the answer might appear to come in the disguise of another problem. For example, you notice a woman at the school gates is having problems starting her car, and even though you are in a hurry, you stop to help her. Your angels might have instigated this meeting for you both. Together you solve the problem and become friends. One day your friend tells you she is starting a child-minding business. You, meanwhile, have just taken on a new job and need someone to take care of your children. So there you have it, another problem solved – but if you hadn't stopped to help that day you would have missed the opportunity. Helping others is always a good thing! Being open and aware to angelic assistance in different ways is how it works.

I do occasionally get messages from people who tell me that they ask their angels for help and it never arrives. They tell me that they've been asking for help for years and it never works. However, when they share their situations it soon becomes clear that angels were working alongside them the whole time! Angels are always with us and always support us.

Years ago, if we needed things, we would put up a simple 'Wanted' advert in the local post office window. These days we have useful things like Freecycle, craigslist or Gumtree – areas where people post things on the internet that they want to get rid of for free or a cash donation (if you have something you want to get rid of, it's also worth doing a swap). By advertising these needs you are projecting your request out into the universe, and maybe angels work with technology now, too! I'm sure they do.

Now, let's look at some more stories!

Chapter 5

Not Asleep

As we've already seen in previous stories, you don't have to be asleep for a loved one to visit from the other side. Although being awake when this happens can be a little unsettling, the healing aspects of the experience still work just the same. A visit is a visit, no matter how it occurs.

I loved Dawn's true story. She told me that it all started when she was pregnant with her daughter. Her mother-in-law was very involved with the pregnancy – this was going to be her first grandchild. Dawn was four or five days late with the birth, and before she was admitted to hospital, her mother-in-law was taken ill and admitted into hospital herself. The family were devastated to discover that the grandma-to-be had cancer.

Dawn promised her mother-in-law that she would be the first to know when the baby was born, and all the other details, like how much the baby weighed. The nurses even took a photo for her. However, when Dawn was discharged the next day, she was told by the staff of the hospital that they would have to wait at least twenty-four hours before they could go and show off the baby to the new grandma. Dawn laughed at the use of the word 'grandma', because her mother-in-law was not keen on it! Dawn called her daughter Ellen and on the Sunday following the birth, she and her partner went to the hospital so that the new grandmother could finally meet the little one. When they were settled at her bedside it was obvious that even though she was so unwell, Dawn's mother-in-law wanted to hold the new baby. Dawn lifted Ellen out of the carrycot so she could have a cuddle.

Sadly, soon after this the older woman took a turn for the worse and the medicines they gave her at the hospital kept her in a coma for most of the time. One night Dawn's partner and his sister went to stay overnight to be with their mother. Dawn was a little on edge because it was her first night alone with Ellen, but she knew it was important the two visited their mother.

The new mum was fine, and as soon as her daughter was sound asleep in her cot, she whispered goodnight to her and went to bed. Then something strange happened. She was woken by the sound of somebody walking into the bedroom. She could hear a noise by the cot! Dawn was shocked to see her daughter's grandma standing by the newborn, saying goodbye. The woman then turned her head slightly towards Dawn, and she felt her say, 'Yes, l couldn't carry on anymore. l had to let go. I couldn't handle the cancer anymore.' Then she was gone as suddenly as she had appeared. Dawn swears she was wide awake when the whole thing happened.

These stories are a double-edged sword, really. And by that I mean they are always sad as well as comforting. It's comforting after the loss of a loved one if they appear from the other side, but nothing is quite the same as having them in the same dimension! We still want them with us, even if we know they are safely in another place.

Joanne's experiences have also occurred while she's been wide awake. Her husband, Dave, died at just forty years of age. The evening before his funeral his wife went back to the flat to pick up a dress to wear. Her mum and dad arrived at 8 p.m., and she opened the front door, holding it wide to let them in. As she did so she spotted a large white feather high up in the sky. Immediately Joanne said, 'I'm getting that, it's for me.' Then she walked outside, put up her hand and the feather flew at an angle straight into her open palm! Joanne's mum said she would never have believed it if she hadn't seen it with her own eyes. Although she didn't believe in the afterlife until that night, afterwards she found many feathers of her own.

Sadly, Joanne explained that her mum passed way just eight months after her husband's transition, and she knows when she is around because she tickles her left arm. Spirits have a way of doing that! I often feel my hair moving up and down. I've even watched it in the mirror, because it seemed so weird I wanted to check it wasn't my imagination. Joanne says Dave comes to her right side and was with her for a year after he died. It's very comforting to know our loved ones live on and come by to see us in this way! Don't ever be frightened by a loving touch from a spirit. They just want to reassure us they are close by.

This next experience is from Australia. Johanna told me her son has visited her numerous times since he passed away; in each instance she was awake when it happened. She explained that she's lived in Australia for forty-one years, having emigrated with her husband and ten-month-old son. Tragically, her son Andy took his own life at just twenty-eight, and Johanna was naturally devastated. She explained her unusual experience to me by saying that a few days before she contacted me, she'd popped into the kitchen to make a cup of coffee, but when she turned round she saw Andy standing there holding a rose. 'This is for you, Ma,' he told her, and promptly vanished!

About five years ago, Johanna lived in a different suburb. She saw a car driving very slowly along the road and inside it was her boy. He was looking out of the window and waving at her. He also appeared at his own funeral – he was above the altar, telling his mum, 'Lighten up, Ma. Lighten up … Look.' Then he did a sort of dance and was singing! Heaven seems such a wonderful place to the departed (when it's their time to leave) that I think they don't understand what it's like for those of us left behind! These little insights can be helpful though.

Johanna was also kind enough to tell me about a near-death experience she'd had. She explained how she was floating above a body, which was lying on a bed. The body seemed to have nothing to do with her, even though it actually belonged to her. I once had an out-of-body experience where I could see my own body lying on the bed. I had little interest in the body because I knew that the 'real me' was the spirit floating over the top of the bed!

Johanna was floating up near the ceiling and remembers she was around twenty at the time it happened. She recalls going up through the ceiling and entering a revolving tunnel. She sat down in the middle of the tunnel because she felt 'so tired in every way possible'. Then a man came along and told her that she had to go to the light. Maybe the 'man' felt that Johanna had died, because usually the spirits of those who have physically died go in that direction. Johanna explained that the light looked a million miles away – it was just a pinprick in the distance. She told him that she wasn't able to move because of her tiredness, and she started crying. People seemed attracted to the crying, maybe because they wanted to know what was going on. Then the man realised that Johanna wasn't dying; she was unwell. He reminded her that she was actually at home and needed help because she was very ill. Next, she felt herself being carried towards the light, but then she was sent back again because the beings told her she wasn't expected. In other words, it wasn't her time to die.

At this point Johanna could hear three voices behind the light. The light was very bright, but not blinding. A voice on the left said she should stay because she'd had such a hard life. A voice on the right said she should go back because her work hadn't been completed. Another voice, in the middle, told her to go for a walk while they made a decision. Next, Johanna instantly found herself beside a river. People were sitting on the riverbank, reading, talking or just hanging around by themselves. She walked along a footpath and the feeling of complete peace and love was overwhelmingly beautiful. The colours were indescribable, so vibrant.

All too soon she found herself in front of the light again – the decision had been made. They told her she had to go back because her life mission had not been completed. Johanna didn't want to go back! 'I went back down that tunnel kicking and screaming! I wanted to stay where I was,' she told me. People asked what was going on, and Johanna shouted that it wasn't fair that she was being sent back to earth.

When she settled down into her body again, she went back to sleep. When she woke up some time later she was unable to move her right arm or leg, or to speak. It turned out that Johanna had survived a massive stroke, and what followed was a complete nervous breakdown. Luckily, she tells me that her health did improve a little over the years.

I wonder if this mystical experience helped Johanna to cope with the life ahead. It does show that our experiences (both good and bad, to us) have meaning. They are part of our life plan; the things that happen to us aren't random, and some of the stories people share do suggest that we have a big say in what these experiences might be (before our souls come to earth!). We help to choose a specific life with particular happenings, which best help us to learn the lessons we've come here for.

Caroline is from Ireland and her experience of a waking visitation is extraordinary. The end of her story is breathtaking, and she has the photographs to prove it! She told me that the last time she saw her dad she knew it was going to be their final meeting. She travelled back to Ireland with her partner and daughter after spending three months with her family in England.

Her dad was recovering from a huge stroke, which had left him unable to speak; he couldn't do anything, really. Sometimes it seemed as if he wasn't even there at all. He was only sixty-three. Caroline told me that, up until that point, he'd been pretty healthy all his life, so it had come as a terrible shock. There seemed to be some hope in the first five weeks or so, but then he had a second big stroke, and after that he would just stare into space or sleep.

After long and careful consideration, and with the support of her family, they made the really difficult decision to go home to Ireland, with the intention of returning to England if anything changed. Caroline's daughter was only four at the time and was starting school in September, so they hoped things might be better by then.

As she said goodbye to her dad she tried so hard to stay positive and humorous around him (you always wonder if they can still hear you). But as she explained to him that the family were leaving, he suddenly turned his head and looked right into her face. His eyebrows were raised, as if he was about to say, 'Yes?' Caroline said she was stunned, and it made her feel nice, but sad at the same time.

Nothing changed at first, but then four or five weeks later her dad took a turn for the worse and the family were left in a real quandary. Caroline told me that her partner was out of work at the time, so they couldn't afford to all visit again so soon. Then the following day she had a really strange experience. It was about nine in the evening and she was lying on her bed, looking out of the window at the sky. Like me, Caroline is a big fan of clouds and often takes photos of them. The colours of the sky that evening were amazing, and she had the urge to grab her camera and go outside to take some pictures. It was an odd feeling, really, because part of her didn't feel in the mood – it was a strange conflict of emotions. In the end, the urge was so great that she followed through with it.

Outside, she lined up the camera to take shots of the sky against a nearby mountain range and then headed back inside again. The urge returned and she felt she simply had to put them onto the computer straight away, which by her own admission she rarely does. As soon as the images loaded, Caroline flicked through them, but she was disappointed. The beautiful colours she'd seen in the sky didn't appear on the photographs, and she felt as if the entire exercise had been pointless.

Then, when she got to the last one, she just froze. Right in the middle of the screen was a face. It was so clear. It was her dad. The only way she could describe it was that it looked like it was embossed onto the clouds – not like the clouds had arranged to make the face, but like the face was coming through them. Caroline couldn't stop smiling because she was so amazed. She showed her partner straight away and he was just as speechless as she was. There was just no denying it.

Caroline's dad passed away the following day, and although Caroline was unable to be with him, her mum, brother and sister were all there right to the end. She believes it was his way of helping her to understand that death is not the end. The family all agree that the photograph is the most amazing gift from heaven.

Chapter 6

Heavenly Visits

When they visit from the other side our mystical friends can sometimes bring strange phenomena with them. Gerri told me that when she was a young child she would often wake up in the early hours of the morning. She says she was always kept occupied by the sound of a male-voice choir singing with great gusto. When she mentioned it to her mum she was told it was the angels singing in heaven. Sadly, when she was old enough to begin school the choir sounds stopped coming.

Susan also got in touch with a similar experience. She explained that she was sitting at home reading when her cat, who'd been sleeping, quickly sat up and started tilting her head as if she was listening to something. All of a sudden Susan, too, heard something she described as a beautiful heavenly choir. There was no TV on, so her first thought was to get up to check if the neighbours were playing music. Susan found nothing, but at the same time she began to feel really uplifted and happy. She recalls feeling very blessed and a lot more positive, as if all her troubles were now behind her. She felt so moved by the experience, she even wrote a poem about it afterwards!

A lady called Linda also shared her angel-music experience with me. She explained how, one morning in the summer of 1994, she was awake early. At the time she had two young children, and they were sleeping soundly. Linda sat up in bed, just looking out of the window at the sunrise – she recalls it must have been about 5:30 a.m. Her room faced east, and she was watching the sun come up over the horizon and over the school that her children would later attend. As she was sitting there she became aware of singing. At first she thought it was one of her own children playing music in the house. She checked but could find no obvious source for the sound.

Linda sat back on the bed and felt an overwhelming sense of peace and love. She describes the music as choir-like – with voices, no instruments, but so beautiful. It continued for about ten minutes, and at the same time a sparkly light appeared in the sky between the two rows of houses opposite. Linda watched closely; it was entrancing.

Once the sun had fully risen the music faded out; the angelic choir had gone. Linda says that the music was 'otherworldly' and like nothing she'd heard before or since. Her belief is that she was serenaded by angelic voices that beautiful summer's morning, and I'm sure she's right. I wonder if this sound is playing all around us all the time, or could it be tied in with the morning sunrise? Perhaps, on occasion (sometimes for no particular reason), we just tune in.

Years ago, when my daughter was unwell, I called out for the angels to help her (well, actually, I was a tired and grumpy mummy and my request was almost rude, but the angels clearly forgave me!). I immediately heard the sound of an angelic choir but didn't immediately understand the gift I had been brought. I searched the whole house, looking for the source of this magical sound. My logical mind found it hard to understand that what I was hearing was a real phenomenon. It took several minutes before I realised that the choir sound was coming from nowhere, but it was all around my daughter. The angels must have done the trick, because my daughter slept soundly all night long, and in the morning she was completely better.

Have you ever heard music from the angels? I wonder if our angels protect us in this way. Many adults have told me that afterlife experiences were very frequent when they were young, and then many years went by when nothing happened at all. If they are lucky, the experiences return when they're adults.

'Why do our loved ones visit from heaven?' some people ask. What is the point of them popping back from the other side? Even Jesus himself came back from the afterlife to reassure the disciples that he was OK. Humankind has always been fascinated with the idea of an afterlife.

We have cave drawings thousands of years old that depict ancient humans' idea of a heavenly realm. Did some early cavemen go to heaven and back and then draw what they had experienced? Then, as now, people had near-death and out-of-body experiences, mystical episodes during sleep or perhaps during rest or relaxation (meditation) periods, and they would have shared those experiences with people they knew. By accident or otherwise, ancient tribes would have imbibed hallucinogenic substances that might also have given them spiritual experiences in which they encountered angels, spirits, alien beings or even God. Do these legends emerge from real encounters? I personally believe they do.

I've studied many past phenomena to see how they relate to the modern day and have found that they have changed very little over the years, if at all. Nowadays we know that visits from the afterlife are surprisingly common.

These are the main reasons why spirits visit us:

- They love us and want us to know that love is unconditional.
- We are supported and cared for.
- They want us to know that they are with us during times of need. (When we might be

worried, scared or perhaps grieving, they draw particularly close to us.) They appear to support us, boost our energy and send us love.

- They appear during important occasions in our lives (weddings, birthdays or anniversaries. They would be aware that you had passed your driving test or high-school diploma).

- They want us to know that death (physical death of the body) only marks the beginning of another form of life. There is no 'death' in the way we understand it.

- They want us to stop worrying about them. They want to reassure us that they are happy where they are.

- Sometimes they feel the need to assure us that others (family members, friends, pets, etc.) are with them and that they have all met up again.

- They want us to know that everything will work out OK (sometimes even giving detailed information about the outcome of a situation, even though they might not really be permitted to do so following the strict universal laws of non-interference!). Our loved ones love us; they can't help trying to protect us wherever they are!

- They want us to know they are watching over us as if they were our guardian angels.

- They are proud of us and continue to take an interest in what we are doing.

- They want us to be happy and to 'carry on' without them, not just coping but thriving in our lives.

Edwina's story illustrates just how much the spirits want to help us. She was going through a particularly difficult time three years ago. She was diagnosed with a very aggressive cancer of the oesophagus. It was a terrible shock, she told me, especially as she was very careful with her health. Edwina was a complementary therapist. She was a vegetarian who ate well and drank very little.

Because she was already on a spiritual path, she called on her angels to help her, and while everyone around her was in shock, Edwina suddenly felt very calm. She says she had a sort of inner knowledge that all would be well. The week before her life-saving surgery, she ordered a book for her husband from an internet bookshop. It arrived the morning of the hospital appointment, but as she opened the package she noticed something unusual. Along with the book she'd ordered for her husband, there was a second book she hadn't ordered (or paid for). *An Angel Held My Hand* (one of my own books) was in the package too. Edwina was stunned. It wasn't mentioned on any of the paperwork, but right away she knew it was sent as a sign that the angels would be with her throughout the ordeal.

A Gift from Heaven

Edwina's operation went well and every day she was in hospital she felt the touch of angels as she meditated and thanked them. Even her surgeon remarked on how calm she was during the whole experience. What a wonderful gift of love!

I'm glad to report that this lovely lady is now fully recovered and very happy, and she feels blessed for the help she received (I hope she enjoyed reading the book too!). I know it sounds funny but, over the years, several people have told me about unusual ways that my angel books (and other people's) have appeared to them. Sometimes they have fallen at people's feet as they were browsing in a bookshop, or come off a shelf as they were trying to look at something different. Angels have this uncanny way of drawing our attention to something we need. They like to bring us information in a subtle, gentle and non-frightening way, but occasionally they can be a little more dramatic if the need arises. As we can see, angels sometimes use my books to get people's attention – and they aren't even on my payroll! ☺

Chapter 7

Hello Again from Heaven

After so many years, it seems no stranger to me that a deceased loved one could visit from heaven than that a living relative might pop round for a cup of tea. With experience, these visits seem normal to me. We know why they visit, but I thought you might be interested in understanding more about how.

The deceased love to bring us signs that they are around. As I mentioned earlier, a white feather is probably the most common and recognisable of these signs, and I've shared white-feather gift stories in numerous books. Other signs might include flickering lights, setting off alarms and playing musical instruments. They might arrange for your (or their) favourite song to play on the radio or for their initials to appear on a car number plate, just moments after you think of them. Sometimes they leave small gifts, like the penny in the next story.

Mike feels that his grandpa has two main ways of visiting him, and he always senses his presence.

A Gift from Heaven

Sometimes when he is typing he accidentally spells out 'Mikie' (his grandpa's name for him) instead of Mike. When this happens he happily accepts the 'accidental' mistake and says 'Hello, Grandpa' in response.

Mike also finds a lot of pennies, and for some reason they are always 'tails up'. Mike felt it was bad luck to pick up a tails-up penny. (There is another saying that suggests you should always pick up a penny because it's actually good luck.) Mike's wife, Gloria, found it amusing, so she'd just laugh and pick up the penny anyway. Mike often felt that it was his grandpa leaving them as gifts.

Then Mike and Gloria stopped in Cheyenne, Wyoming, to 'freshen up' Grandpa and Grandma's graves (which Mike says they do several times a year). True to form, when they walked up to the gravestone they saw, neatly placed in the lower right-hand corner, a penny … tails up, of course!

The most common sign of my own, and my favourite, is when my loved ones reach out to me when I am asleep. I've loved sharing these stories with you over the years. They always enchant me, never stop amazing me and continue to comfort me.

Margaret has experienced these kinds of encounters, too. She lost her husband to throat cancer, so he hadn't been able to speak well for a while before he passed over. One night, he appeared to her in a very real dream. Margaret could hear the shower going (although she didn't have one in the place she now lived), then she heard it switch off and the door of the bathroom opened. Out walked her husband. He was wearing shorts, an open shirt and a towel wrapped around his neck.

'All right, mate,' he said, and smiled at his wife. Margaret was stunned but replied that she was. With that, he turned and walked into the kitchen. Margaret followed her husband but, unsurprisingly, he wasn't there. At that point she woke up, and even though she found the experience comforting, she told me she just cried, because she was so over-whelmed by it. I used to do this a lot myself in the early days. People become emotional because the experiences seem so real – because, of course, they are real. I've actually woken up with real tears in my eyes. I've also felt my late father's hand in mine, and as I've woken up I've still felt it for several moments afterwards.

Here is a clever dream visitation. With only moments in which to establish an idea or message, Rebecca's mum decided to use a sort of code. Her mum passed away in 2010, and after about nine months her daughter had a dream-visitation experience. She recalls asking her mum what it was like where she was (in heaven), hoping she might give her some insight into it all, but she never spoke a word. Cleverly, what she did instead was draw on Rebecca's left hand in black pencil. When she looked at her hand, Rebecca found that her mother had marked out an Egyptian symbol of a head!

The 'dream' was the clearest and most memorable she'd ever experienced. She felt right away that her mum was giving her a clue or a sign as to where she was residing. As the Egyptian people were very much interested in life after death, Rebecca felt it indicated that the afterlife was a real place. I did some follow-up research myself and discovered that a head featuring in a dream usually symbolises 'an idea' or 'thought or intellect'. A pencil in a dream just means communication (as she was communicating the idea of the afterlife to her daughter). Hands usually mean something like, 'You can handle this,' and the left might mean that something could be 'left' behind (or perhaps a worry of being 'left' out). Have you ever had a dream with clues like this? Rebecca told me that she has never experienced anything like it before or since.

Over the years I've read numerous stories that seem to indicate that the deceased know it's their time to pass over to the other side. What do you think about this one? Wyn wrote to me after reading my book *An Angel by My Side*. She already believed that her sister Lilian had psychic abilities, but when Lilian passed away, she almost seemed to be announcing to the family, or warning them, when it was going to happen.

Sadly, Lilian had been battling liver cancer and had been told there was nothing more the doctors could do for her. Lilian was in hospital waiting to come home when she told her family that her (deceased) parents had 'come for her' the night before but she'd turned them away, saying she wasn't ready. Perhaps at this time Lilian decided on a suitable date with them, because she kept mentioning 'Thursday' to her son. She came home on the Monday, and Wyn was sitting in the bedroom with her on Tuesday when suddenly she announced, 'It'll have to be Thursday.' When Wyn asked her sister what she meant by this she just repeated the phrase again. Lilian died at 12:10 a.m. … on the Thursday!

It's always tragic when our loved ones pass on, at any age, but what is special about Wyn's story is that the sisters' deceased parents came to collect Lilian. We had a similar experience in our family. A few weeks before my own father passed away, he was in hospital when his aunt and grandfather came to 'collect him'. Dad turned them away, I'm guessing because he, too, wasn't ready. Dad lived a few weeks longer, just enough time for the family to spend Christmas together and for him and Mum to enjoy their Christmas present from the family – a weekend trip to London to see a musical: *Joseph*, Dad's favourite!

Not everyone is lucky enough to be consciously aware of these final choices. If we're really and truly honest, I'm not sure we're ever ready to let our loved ones go, even if it seems like deep down inside the soul may know when 'their time' really is and why.

Some of the many experiences I've heard about show loved ones popping over to see us just to say goodbye. This happens a lot when relatives haven't been able to say it in life. Of course, we never know when a visit will be 'the last time', but this causes many people great anguish, and the spirit of the deceased seems to be aware of this extra burden we carry.

Michelle's story covers this experience. She kindly began her letter by thanking me for sharing my gift with the world, but I'm always keen to point out that I love what I do and it's my pleasure! Michelle lost her dad a couple of days before she wrote to me, so her experience was very fresh in her mind. Her dad had a massive heart attack a week after having surgery on his spine. He was put on a life-support machine and recovered a few days later; he was up and talking to everyone like nothing had happened. Michelle's dad lived in Eastbourne (he moved there when Michelle was a baby), and the rest of the family lived in Liverpool.

After the heart attack, Michelle's nan, aunties and uncles travelled to be with him, but as her husband couldn't get any time off work, he and Michelle decided to join the rest of the family at the weekend. They wanted to surprise her dad. Michelle says they got out their sat nav, ready to go to the hospital that weekend, but sadly it was too late – an aunty phoned to tell them that Dad had experienced a secondary heart attack and had already passed away. Michelle, quite naturally, was left devastated that she'd been unable to see her dad one last time, but her dad clearly had other plans.

That night, Michelle was having a normal dream when her dad popped in as a spirit visitation. He wanted to say he loved her. He apologised and explained that he 'had to go'. So clear was the experience that she even described to me what he was wearing. It's funny how these details are important.

A couple of days later, when Michelle and her husband should have been driving to see her dad, she was watching an old episode of *Touched by an Angel* (the TV show about an angel helping humans) when the sat nav, which was sitting on the side, suddenly said 'turn left'. Michelle was in complete shock because, as she explained, firstly it was completely dead (not charged, not switched on), secondly it didn't receive a signal until you got outside the house and thirdly no destination was typed into it. Michelle believes it was another sign from her dad, probably letting her know he'd reached his destination. Isn't this fabulous? Never underestimate how clever spirits are.

* * *

A Gift from Heaven

The love that exists between worlds never ends. Death of the physical body doesn't mean the end of the relationship with the lost loved one. Clearly our connection to the deceased has changed (as I typed that my spare phone on the desk in front of me bleeped for no obvious reason!). It's easy to say that we never see them again, yet many thousands (and possibly millions) of people do have experiences where they see the spirits of their lost loves in dream-visitation-type experiences. We could say that we never get to touch them again, yet many of the stories in my books contain examples of people hugging, holding hands and even dancing together (see my book *Call Me When You Get to Heaven*).

As we have seen, after death our loved ones still take an interest in our lives, turning up at important events like weddings, celebrations and the birth of new family members. When they first cross over, many are met by others who have passed before, and I've shared many such stories in my other books. The deceased appear to us (or at least communicate that they are around us) when we are stressed, depressed or grieving. Their many signs include butterflies, birds, notices, flickering lights and other electronic phenomena. Their ability to reach out to us knows no boundaries.

Sometimes experiences happen after folk have read several books of other people's angel and afterlife experiences. It's as if they, the deceased, want us to be prepared (and don't want us to be frightened) before they make the epic journey from one world to another. To reach out to us they have to cross through another dimension, but many work hard to do so in whatever way they can. I'm sure it's as difficult for them to visit our realm as it is for us to visit theirs.

I love sharing stories of our angels and of afterlife communication and interaction. There is more to our world than you can possibly believe. What we see, hear and feel with our mortal bodies doesn't even begin to scratch the surface of 'what is'. Keep an open mind; ask for your loved ones to reach out to you or share a sign and you might well be surprised at what you experience.

In this final story I want to show you one last connection. Although our loved ones make an effort to reach out to us, sometimes we don't make the connection, or perhaps our grieving prevents us from experiencing it for some reason. When this happens, your loved ones don't give up; they will try to reach out to someone else with the message. Sometimes this might be a professional psychic (a medium), other times it might be a friend or relative (or even a neighbour), and at other times your message might come from a total stranger.

Jonathan told me he felt compelled to write and share his experience after reading one of my books.

A Gift from Heaven

At the time he was mourning the loss of his mum, who'd passed away unexpectedly. Jonathan is an experienced nurse working for the National Health Service, but he says nothing could ever have prepared him for the soul-searching pain he felt. There was, however, an experience he had back in the 1990s that gave him some glimmer of peace.

Jonathan remembers being asked to take charge of a nursing home, which was 30 miles from where he lived. He says he knew no one and, as he'd recently lost his gran, he was quieter than normal. Jonathan decided not to tell anyone that night about his loss, knowing that it would be easier to remain professional if he grieved in private. Yet in the morning, something very strange happened. He was 'handing over' to the day nurse when a woman came through the front door and walked right up to him. The woman, dressed in an auxiliary uniform, was unknown to him, but she spoke to him and said, 'I have a message for you. Your gran visited me last night and asked me to tell you she wants you to stop mourning and to live your life, and she wants you to know that she will always be with you.' Jonathan was completely stunned. No one could possibly have known about the loss, could they? Gran might have popped over from the other side with the intention of visiting her grandson directly in his dream, but working the night shift meant that Jonathan was awake at the time of the visit. Clever Gran did the next best thing and got the message to her loving relative anyway.

And so, dear reader, we have come to the end of another collection of angel and afterlife stories, but I've many other books for you to enjoy. I love to read my fans' amazing stories too. I'm interested in paranormal experiences of any sort, so if you'd like to get in touch, I'd love to hear from you. Who knows? You might end up in a future book (with your permission, of course).

If you'd like to share your stories with me, there is a contact page on my website. If you have questions about your experiences, as my readers often do, then you are most welcome to follow me on my various networking sites (for the direct links, visit my website). I will do my best to help you and answer your questions. Like your own guardian angel, I'm always here for you. Thank you for reading.

Much love and angel blessings,
Jacky Newcomb
'The Angel Lady' x

www.JackyNewcomb.com

Moving Memoirs

Stories of hope, courage and the power of love…

If you loved this book, then you will love our Moving Memoirs eNewsletter

Sign up to…

- Be the first to hear about new books

- Get sneak previews from your favourite authors

- Read exclusive interviews

- Be entered into our monthly prize draw to win one of our latest releases before it's even hit the shops!

Sign up at

www.moving-memoirs.com